Roman Mythology

Tales From the Roman Pantheon

Adam Andino

Table of Contents

Introduction: A Brief History of Roman Mythology

Veni. Vidi. Vici. "I came. I saw. I conquered."

Julius Caesar, the first emperor of Rome and warmonger, wrote one of the most iconic Latin phrases known to humans after conquering Gaul around 47 BCE, thus expanding the empire even more. His reputation precedes him, even almost two millennia later. As impressive as Caesar's military career was, the city of Rome and its people had been settled in the area for hundreds of years before him and continued until the fall of the Roman Empire.

The Roman Empire's collapse is highly debated in historical circles. Some say it fell with the rise of the Byzantine Empire in 476 CE, others say it fell in the 15th century when Constantinople, in modern-day Istanbul, Turkey did.

Why did the Roman Empire fall? Its theories are numerous, including the rise of Islam, lead in the drinking water, inflation with other economic problems, and even allowing vandals and barbarians to have positions of power. By far the most popular and widely believed is the rise of Christianity. Beforehand, Rome's main religion was polytheistic, or involved the worshiping of many gods. It was the lifeblood of the Roman belief systems and culture. This culture dated back thousands of years, as far back enough to when the Etruscans were in power.

Greek and Latin Influences

The original Romans were not called Romans but were a part of a small hub of villages settled in the area known as Latium. These people were known as the Latins, and they were known to be extremely superstitious and believed in many gods, goddesses, and spirits. Their main concerns at the time were for the deities to watch over the farm and the home. Over time, the hub became a city and eventually made contact with the Greeks. The Greek influence on the Latins was immense. The Latins and Greeks were both polytheistic and had many deities ruling over the same element or power. The Latins recognized this, and to differentiate between the two religions, kept their Latin names. For example, the Greek god Zeus is known as Jupiter in Roman mythology today.

While it may seem that Greek and Roman mythology are the same to the untrained eye, the Romans do have their own unique myths and legends. For example, Rome has a long and complicated saga of its founding: From Aeneas fleeing the Trojan War to Romulus and Remus, Rome has found a way to stand out from its Greek predecessors. Some of the deities' origins are from the Etruscans, with one of the earliest gods known as Janus.

Janus has no Greek equivalent, as this particular deity predated the intervention of the Greeks.

Tolerant Religion

Many polytheistic religions, past or present, were surprisingly very tolerant of other religions. With the exception of Christianity and the persecution of Jews at the turn of the millennium, the Romans, in regard to religion, have had few atrocities committed for the sake of a following. For example, rarely were there any human sacrifices. While the Romans expanded their empire, they drew inspiration from the localized deities of the area. An example would be Isis, the Egyptian goddess of the earth. Instead of forgoing the religion altogether, they instead constructed temples in her name and integrated her within their realm of deities.

How the Gods Impacted Daily Living

Religion had a massive impact on the daily living of the Romans, although it was not directly implemented into their laws to maintain order. Since religion had been so ingrained into the society of the Latins, it was naturally a driving force in the Roman society as well. There was no formal code on how to conduct themselves, unlike in other religious texts such as the

Bible. The rituals and beliefs of the importance of the farm and home were well established before the future complexities of Rome.

Worshiping the Deities

While the Romans had no official code of conduct, they worshiped their deities in regard to what they needed in their lives. A couple wanting to have a child would pray to Juno, the goddess of fertility; a farmer would pray to the goddess of agriculture Ceres for a year of plentiful crops. Each god or goddess had its purpose. Temples were constructed in each of the gods' names. No expense was spared in creating the temples, especially those of the 12 main deities of the pantheon. They were complete with priests who served the temple of the god, such as Jupiter or Minerva. The priests would then interpret signs and omens they believed were sent from the gods and help those in need of counsel.

Further strengthening their connection to the gods, the Romans had many celebrations and rituals throughout the year. One of the most popular traditions celebrated to this day was called *Saturnalia* and falls on December 17th to celebrate winter solstice. With each new introduction of governments, such as the Republic, the Augustan Empire, and the reign of Caligula, the once one-day celebration expanded into a holiday of joy and eventual roughhousing. It was also to pay homage to the god of agriculture, Saturn. Sacrifices of pigs at the Temple of Saturn kicked off the beginning of the festivities the night before the festival and then were served the next day as everyone feasted. Copious amounts of wine were consumed, gambling laws were lax, and slaves were relieved of duties for the celebration. Trees with leaves still green decorated the city, complete with lit lanterns and candles at night. As was part of the tradition, small gifts were given and received by friends, family, and acquaintances.

While Saturnalia was just one of the many festivals in Ancient Rome, it was a reminder of the power the gods possessed. The presence of the gods was constantly felt throughout daily life, ranging from prayers, to offerings at a temple, to times of merriment for numerous celebrations and holidays. Most of the gods were celebrated, and some were even feared to deter any bad moral principles. However, the main gods of the pantheon reigned supreme.

Chapter 1: The 12 Main Gods and Goddesses

The main gods and goddesses of the Roman pantheon ruled the overworld, commanding authority in the Romans' lives. These gods and goddesses reigned supreme and were the most worshiped among the deities. They are also the most well-known throughout history.

Apollo: God of the Sun

Apollo, while known as the god of the sun, he also was designated as the god of music, healing, agriculture, and prophecy. Many stories revolved around both his ferocity and gentleness. As one of the (many) sons of Jupiter and a mother of mortal origin, along with his twin sister, Diana, the complexities of his personality were not surprising. It is said that some of the other gods were afraid of his bouts of anger. Apollo's name is the same in both Greek and Roman mythologies—the only main god to have this distinction.

Ceres: Goddess of Agriculture

Ceres was the goddess of agriculture, fertility, and the harvest, and she was the matriarch of the family. In her generosity, she granted the gift of agriculture to the farmers, who then learned to feed their families, therefore, growing the community. Ceres's mood shifted in the autumn and winter while her daughter, Proserpina, fathered by Jupiter, lived in the Underworld with Pluto, thus causing the crops to wither and die. In the spring and summer, she rejoices in her daughter's return with the arrival of new growth. Ceres's ties to family are important to her. As one of Jupiter's sisters, family is ingrained in her.

Diana: Goddess of the Hunt

In contrast to Apollo, his twin Diana is a reserved, private goddess. She is the goddess of the hunt, the moon, nature, and fertility, but mainly childbirth. She protected women during childbirth as well as provided bountiful hunting for the hunters at night. Her most notable possession is her chariot which dragged the moon and darkness across the sky. Diana's mood affected the moon's size: The smaller the moon, the lazier and moodier she felt.

Juno: Queen of the Gods and Goddess of Fertility

Juno, whose name is forever ingrained in the calendar as June, was the queen of the gods. She was married to her brother,

Jupiter, and is the mother of Vulcan, Mars, Juventas, and Bellona. She was also known as the patron goddess of Rome. As a member of the Capitoline Triad, the three highest-ranking gods in the religion, she reigned over fertility, marriage, and women in general. She was the protector of married women and Rome; however, she was a notoriously jealous and vindictive goddess due to Jupiter's many affairs and illegitimate children.

Jupiter: King of the Gods and God of the Sky

As the king of all the deities, Jupiter reigned over the sky, lightning, and thunder with a thunderbolt in hand. Not only was he god of the sky, but he also oversaw the Romans and protected the state and all the laws that were implemented through the state. He was the youngest of six siblings who led the revolution to free the gods of his father, Saturn's, tyrannical leadership. He and his two brothers divided the realms: Jupiter ruled the skies and appointed himself king, Neptune ruled the sea, and Pluto ruled the Underworld. Jupiter also had three sisters: Juno, whom he later married, Ceres, and Vesta. While beloved by the Romans, his affinity for mortal women and other goddesses often induced Juno's rage and jealousy towards him and the children he fathered. Some of the most known of his children are Hercules, Minerva, Proserpina, Bacchus, Apollo, Diana, Vulcan in some myths, Juventas, Bellona, Mars, and Helen of Troy.

Jupiter, along with Juno and Minerva, are also part of the Capitoline Triad.

Mars: God of War

Mars is the god of war, agriculture, and military power as a means for peace. His bloodlust protected the state and city borders and quashed any skirmishes as the Roman Empire expanded. Juno and Jupiter were his parents, and therefore, his complex personality shone. Mars fathered Romulus and Remus, the founders of the city of Rome, along with Venus and two other children.

Mercury: Messenger of the Gods and God of Finance

As the messenger of the gods, Mercury had many roles to fill. Known for his loyalty, trustworthiness, and winged sandals, he was the swiftest and most cunning of the main gods. He was the god of finance, trickery, thievery, trade, communication, and travel. He was the protector of anything financial: shopkeepers, merchants, and thieves. The messenger of the gods escorted the souls of the dead to the River Styx where they were ferried across to the Underworld.

Minerva: Goddess of Wisdom

Minerva, the goddess of wisdom, craft, trade, and strategy, is one of the most powerful of all the gods. It was believed that Minerva was the favorite of Jupiter's children, as he gave her the remaining position in the Capitoline Triad. She was one of the most revered by gods and mortals alike.

Neptune: God of the Sea

Ancient Rome's version of *Aquaman*, Neptune was the god of both fresh and saltwater. His anger was feared, as it caused heavy storms complete with choppy waters in his rage. He was a famous equestrian and protected the horses and oversaw horse and chariot races with Minerva. His five siblings included his brothers Jupiter and Pluto and his sisters Juno, Ceres, and Vesta.

Venus: Goddess of Love

When it comes to the ultimate goddess of love, Venus was it. Her other epithets included fertility, sex, beauty, and pleasure. She was a child of Jupiter and married to Vulcan, the god of the forge. Her famous love affair with Mars was coveted by many Romans because of their passion and love for one another. She had four children with Mars including Romulus and Remus, but their line is predated by her son Aeneas.

Vesta: Goddess of the Hearth

Rarely depicted in her goddess form, she is the goddess who is symbolically illustrated as a flame. She was the goddess of the hearth and the home. She protected the Roman people and was the remaining sister of Jupiter. An entire cult was named after her called the Vestal Virgins. They dedicated 30 years of their life in service of her sacred temple and to tend the eternal flame presented to a Roman emperor. This flame was to protect Rome from harm, and if it were to extinguish, it was believed that Rome would fall. Vesta's temple was exclusive; only the priestesses were allowed access to pray and tend the flame.

Vulcan: God of the Forge

The remaining main god is Vulcan, the god of the forge, including both craftsmanship and blacksmithing, weaponry, volcanoes, and fire. One of the sons of Jupiter and Juno, he often wielded a hammer to craft the best weapons and guide blacksmiths at the forge. Vulcan was also the husband of Venus.

Chapter 2: Characters and Creatures

Not only were there twelve main gods, but the Romans worshiped a plethora of additional gods and goddesses. While many overlapped in their usefulness, the deities oversaw every aspect of the Romans' lives. Before the introduction of Christianity and, therefore, the Catholic Church, the Romans believed in minor gods, demigods, and hideous creatures to use as a means of teaching morals and virtues, and also to scare children into behaving.

Below are some examples of minor gods, demigods, heroes, and some of the creatures in the Roman pantheon.

Minor Gods

Many of the minor gods held a small level of authority over the lives of Romans. Some of the gods were borrowed from the Greeks, but there are a few strictly Roman-only minor gods. These deities specialized in a small set of skills, while the main gods oversaw the Romans as a whole. Below are a few examples.

Janus: God of Doorways and Transitions

Janus, the god of two faces had the power of seeing into the future and the past. He was represented in an archway located outside of Circo Massimo. As the god with two faces, he represented doorways, transitions, gates, time, duality, beginnings and endings, and passages. He was one of the first-worshipped gods before Greek influence and remained one of the few gods to be strictly Roman. The month of January is named in his honor, as January marks the end of a year and the beginning of a new one. The doors to his temple represented times of war and peace. If the doors were open, peace was upon Rome. If the door was closed, Rome was entering into a world of war.

Nox: Goddess of the Night

Nox sprouted out of Chaos, her parent, and was one of the most ancient of all beings. She was the original goddess of the night and married the god of darkness, Erebus. She was normally depicted either as a goddess in a chariot enshrouded with dark or black mist. Nox was solely responsible for conjuring the Fates, Sleep, Pain, Strife, and Death, among a number of other dark spirits.

Proserpina: Goddess of Fertility

Proserpina, the daughter of Ceres and Jupiter, and wife of the king of the Underworld, Pluto, was the goddess of wine, agriculture, and fertility. While she was mostly known for being abducted by Pluto, she was a goddess to look over the Romans during times of harvest and growing crops. We will discuss more about Proserpina in Chapter 7: The Reason of the Changing Seasons.

Pluto: God of the Underworld

Pluto was the brother of Jupiter and Neptune, who was chosen to be the king of the Underworld. His queen, Proserpina, ruled with him for half of the year. He is the god of death and wealth with an affinity for diamonds, the richest ore known to both gods and humans. In a way, he was also the god of agriculture as he ruled the land deep beneath the earth, watching over the seeds as they grew. In contrast to the Greek depiction of the god Hades, Romans celebrated him as both a wonderful husband to Proserpina and a firm ruler.

Saturn: God of Time

Saturn was the father of six children: Jupiter, Pluto, Ceres, Juno, Neptune, and Vestas, and was overthrown by them in a revolt led by Jupiter. While mainly the god of time, he oversaw wealth, generation, agriculture, and periodic liberation. A feast called Saturnalia was celebrated in his name and ranged from one to five days on December 17th. During the time that Saturn ruled, it was thought that Romans enjoyed a bountiful lifestyle with little to no labor.

Demigods and Heroes

Demigods and heroes fell into a separate category on their own. Each demigod or hero mentioned had deep roots in the lore of Roman mythology and of the founding of Rome itself. They were known to fight off creatures in trials and even to throw parties. Demigods and heroes reminded the Romans to be resilient in their trials and tribulations, especially when it came to their destinies. Below is more information on some of the more famous demigods and heroes, Aeneas, Bacchus, Hercules, Remus, and Romulus.

Aeneas

While Aeneas's story will be covered more in the next chapter, he is primarily renowned as the father and founder of the region Latium, founded while fleeing the Greeks in Troy. As her son, Venus often aided and recruited help for him on his quests. He traveled for six long years to discover a new civilization for his people called the Aeneads. His bloodline was responsible for the founding of Rome: Romulus and Remus.

Romulus and Remus

Remus, along with his twin brother Romulus, were among the long line of founders of Rome. He and Romulus have many myths attached to their name, including their lineage. Their mother, Rhea, was thought to be a descendent of Aeneas and their father was Mars, the god of war. Remus was killed in a dispute with his brother over where to found a new city during their reign. Romulus continued to rule the city dubbed Rome after him, and he continued to rule as king of the Romans until his death.

Bacchus

Bacchus was the Roman god of wine most notably, but he also had his hands in agriculture and fertility. It was said he taught the Romans to make wine by the fermentation of grapes. While still considered a god, his father was Jupiter, and his mother was a mortal. Jupiter was notorious for his affairs with mortal women and gods alike. In the case of Bacchus, however, he was the first to rule with his father in the sky. He notoriously carried a goblet of wine everywhere he went and was the face of public drunkenness.

Hercules

Thanks to Disney's film, *Hercules*, this demigod is famous for his labors and many encounters with Pluto. With Jupiter as his father and his mother a mortal, the main attributes of Hercules were his inhuman physical strength, immeasurable courage, and resourcefulness. With his twelve labors, he was able to make the world safer for regular mortals. Upon his death, he chose to ascend to rule with his father as the god of heroes.

Creatures and Monsters

The creatures and monsters of Roman mythology are one of the many inspirations for the depictions of creatures in today's movies, TV shows, and books. Myriad artists have drawn inspiration from the creatures and monsters to tell their own hero and adventure stories.

Cacus

Cacus was the son of Vulcan and lived in a cave on the future site of Rome, located near Palatine Hill. As a fire-breathing giant who feasted on human flesh, he terrorized the surrounding villages. To rub salt in the human-flesh wound, he nailed the heads of his victims on the door to the entrance of his cave. Cacus was later disposed of by Hercules.

Cyclops

The cyclops in Roman mythology was a giant with a singular bulging eye located directly in the middle of its forehead. While there are several myths surrounding the cyclops, the Roman myth describes how the brother of the cyclops, Saturn, threw them into the Underworld. When Jupiter planned to overthrow his father, he released them from their hellish prison. As repayment, the cyclops fashioned Jupiter his famous lightning bolt and also gave him the gift of thunder. With Vulcan, they forged the weapons of the gods.

Faun

Most commonly known as satyrs, fauns were woodland creatures who typically were present with Bacchus, the god of wine. Normally depicted with a flute, they trotted along the woods without a care in the world. These creatures were chimeras–creatures with qualities of more than one animal. In the case of the fauns, they are half human, half goat. The human parts of the fauns were their torsos, upper limbs, and young faces. Soft curly hair was atop their heads, and they had pointed ears. The goat parts included goat legs complete with hooves, a tail, and horns on their heads.

Hydra

Hercules also killed this creature during his twelve labors. The hydra, most renowned for its many heads and ability to regrow them, was sleek with a massive body of a serpent. It was a guard to the entrance of the Underworld with its lair in the lake of

Lerna. Everything about the hydra was ripe with poison. From its scent to its breath to even its blood, the hydra killed anyone who happened to stumble upon its lair.

Chapter 3: Before the Founding of Rome

Equō nē crēdite, Teucrī! Quidquid id est, timeō Danaōs et dōna ferentēs. "Do not trust the horse, Trojans! Whatever it is, beware the Greeks bearing gifts." Virgil's famous quote from the epic poem *The Aeneid* encompassed the tale of Aeneas fleeing from Troy. While myths and legends were passed through generations of Greek and Romans alike, the myths in this chapter are strictly about the founding of Rome.

The Myth of Janus

In the beginning, hundreds of years before Aeneas, Romulus, and Remus, a ruler named Janus reigned over the land of Latium. A wise ruler, Janus, led them through many years of peace and prosperity in the land. His laws were fair and just. He lived on Janiculum Hill, one of the seven hills that would eventually become Rome.

Janus: The Man Turned God

Saturn, the god of agriculture and time, was recently overthrown by his children, led by Jupiter. In a discouraged state, he encountered Janus on the hill outside of his home. Janus was shocked at the state of Saturn, and as he gazed at the lonely god, a pang of sympathy struck him.

Saturn told the tale of the mutiny of his children. He was heartbroken. Not only had he lost his kingdom, but he grieved for the loss of respect his children had once given him. The god's tale moved Janus; his voice cracked and tightened as he spoke.

Janus wanted to comfort the grieving Saturn, but the god was inconsolable. There was nothing he could say, but soon he realized he could offer something: To share ruling the kingdom together. Although Janus knew it would not bring back the respect of his children and the loss of an entire kingdom, it was the least he could do.

Saturn listened to the proposition and considered it, and then accepted it. In his gratitude, he offered a reward of his own: Janus would be made a god. Janus accepted the gift. Now immortal, his specialty was to see both the past and future. Saturn then ushered in a Golden Era with many years of peace and prosperity.

Conclusion

The myth of Janus represented a god with roots tied directly to the land, leading directly to the future myths and legends of the founding of Rome. The god Saturn rewarded the generosity of

Janus by turning him into a deity and solidifying the region's connection to the gods. By cementing their gods into the foundation of the founding of Rome, the Romans established a strong connection to the land itself.

Cassandra: The Seer No One Believed

The myth of Cassandra and Apollo is set in Greece, presenting the themes of love and betrayal. It is a riveting, classic tale of a love that was not reciprocated, ending with the premonition of the fall of Troy and, thus, the eventual founding of Rome. Several different versions of the myth exist in the world today.

Cassandra and Apollo: A Rejection and a Curse

Cassandra was the strikingly beautiful daughter of King Priam of Troy. She had three brothers: Helenus, her twin, Hector, the hero of Troy, and Paris, who sparked the Trojan War by taking Helen (later known as Helen of Troy) from Sparta as his bride. Her family, being the direct cause of the war, was infamous.

She sat alone outside in Troy when Apollo stopped to admire her. He fell instantly in love with her because of her beauty, as his father Jupiter had done numerous times with multiple women, both goddesses and mortals alike. He enticed her with the promise of the gift of foresight and prophecy. In return, he wanted favors and her loyalty to him.

Although the reasoning behind her rejection of the god was uncertain, the rejection was clear: she did not want him. Some versions of this myth suggest that Cassandra used Apollo to gain the power of prophecy, and then saw the future and Apollo's involvement in the fall of Troy and rejected him because of that. Other myths report that Apollo's repeated advances and the ferocity behind the advances were too much for her to handle.

The rejection enraged Apollo: after all, he had given her the power of foresight. Since the gift was given freely, it could not be lifted. Instead, he cursed her. From that moment on, no matter the precision of the prophecy, nobody would believe her.

Cassandra, The Lunatic

The life of Cassandra was wrought with despair afterward. She often warned her brothers of prophecies of their demise and the downfall of Troy and even begged them not to leave, but they refused to acknowledge her. Paris brought back Helen from Sparta against her warning. She also warned Hector of his impending death. Despite their distrust in her, her prophecies would come to pass.

Labeled as a lunatic and a madwoman who uttered nonsense, her father hid her in a citadel. She was an embarrassment to him, and therefore, could never set foot outside of the citadel. She was guarded day and night, with her father never allowing her to leave.

Years passed as the Trojan War raged on, with each prophecy of hers repeatedly ignored. The infamous Trojan Horse, an assumed gift of the Greeks, was among her greatest failures to keep her people safe. Her famous line about the Greeks within their horse is immortalized in Virgil's epic poem *The Aeneid*: "Beware the Greeks bringing gifts!" In a vain attempt to stop the Greeks, she grabbed a torch and marched to the horse, ready to watch it go up in flames. Several guards caught her and removed the torch from her hands, reprimanding her for burning the gift. Soon, she would watch the city she loved so much become ravaged. The Fall of Troy was imminent.

The Aftermath of Troy

After the fall of Troy, Cassandra sought refuge at the temple of Minerva where a Greek soldier, Ajax, found and kidnapped her. Through the divine intervention of both Minerva and Neptune, Ajax drowned in the depths of the sea. However, her troubles were far from over.

She was then forced to be the concubine of the king of Mycenae known as King Agamemnon who already had a wife back at home. She prophesied his death as well as her own upon arrival to Mycenae. Agamemnon refused to believe her prophecy. While away at war, his wife and her lover had plotted to kill him. Enraged more so that the king had taken a concubine under his wing, the plotting continued until their arrival. The queen's wish was fulfilled, and Cassandra's final prophecy came true.

Conclusion

The myth of Cassandra and Apollo paved the way for the many myths surrounding the origins of Rome. Because no one believed in her prophecies, her and Apollo's direct and indirect involvement in the events surrounding the Trojan War led to Aeneas fleeing Troy, where he then discovered a new place to grow and prosper.

Chapter 4: Aeneas and the Founding of Latium

The myth of Aeneas really begins with his conception. As the result of a coupling of Venus, the goddess of love, and Anchises, a prince of Troy, he was born with a difficult destiny: To lead his people to a new land. Although he would not know his destiny until decades later, he is considered to be one of the original founders of Rome. His childhood and early adult life are a mystery, as the story of Aeneas as told by Virgil did not start until after the fall of Troy.

The Fall of Troy

After the Trojan Horse was brought inside the city walls, Troy fell during the night. Aeneas, along with Hector, held his ground as the Greeks poured into the city. He and Hector held them for as long as they could before realizing their attempts were futile. Hector told him of a vision where his destiny was not to die there fighting off the Greeks, but to found another city outside of Greece.

After heeding the vision of Hector, Aeneas attempted to find his wife, but she had disappeared inside the burning chaos of Troy. He grabbed his son Ascanius, his father, and other soldiers and survivors who were attempting to flee. Aeneas also took with him some of the gods of Troy, which were small statues that would later be restated in the new city. He then led what remained of his family and the band of survivors away from the destruction while the Greeks sacked the city. The surviving band of survivors called the Aeneads, made their way to safety on the ships that were docked at the harbor.

After they escaped, the Aeneads sailed along the Mediterranean. His wife's ghost appeared to him, telling him of his destiny, and gave him a direction and destination: Head west and look for what is now known as the Tiber River. With this new destination in mind, they began their long journey to the new land.

The Chronicles of Greece

They first sailed to Thrace in Greece, where he buried Polydorus, who was the son of King Priam. The soil oozed from the blood of the Trojan War. With his last breath, Polydorus informed Aeneas that Thrace was not the place for him and his crew. After they buried him, the Aeneads continued on their quest.

The next stop was Delos, still in Greece. Apollo met with Aeneas, and advised him to keep going. Delos was not where his ancestors lay. So, off he and the Aeneads sailed.

They continued to visit varying places in Greece, each less promising than the last. First, Crete, where Aeneas had a vision that his ancestors were not present. Then, the Strophades Islands, where they were attacked by harpies. The Aeneads beat the harpies, with the last of them telling him their final destination was Italy.

In Actium, they continued the tradition of the Trojan Games, which was supposedly created by an ancestor of Julius Caesar as a way to display the skills of both his soldiers and their horseback riding skills. The games were a distraction and a welcome break for the Aeneads. After their break, they sailed to Buthrotum and met the wife of Hector, named Andromache.

After sailing for several years, they drifted from Ceraunia on the eastern coast of Italy, across the Adriatic Sea and west to Sicily. In Sicily, they glimpsed at Mount Etna for the first time while staying in the harbor of the cyclops. It was here that they met Achaemendies, who blinded the cyclops, taking him in as a member of their crew. The father of Aeneas died, which prompted them to leave Sicily in their grief. Although there was a shorter route, it was littered with enemy Greek ships. Not wanting to face a battle they could not win; they headed further south.

Juno's Interference: A Shipwreck and a Love Affair

Juno, who was in favor of the Greeks, was not pleased with Aeneas fleeing Troy to found a new city. In her fury, she demanded that Aelous, the god of wind, create a storm to prevent them from reaching their final destination. The storm raged. Treacherous waters and escalating waves almost ended the destiny of Aeneas. Neptune, realizing that the storm was not of his own making and knowing of the destiny of the Aeneads, calmed the storm enough to grant safe passage to the next spot: Carthage.

The Aeneads, exhausted and shipwrecked, sought refuge on the coast of Africa in Carthage, or modern-day Tunisia. So far, their journey had culminated in six years of voyaging, desperate to find their new home. The beaten crew was granted refuge while they recuperated.

Fatigued by their treacherous journey, many members of the crew wanted to stay. With the help of Juno and his mother, Venus, Aeneas fell in love with the Carthaginian queen, Dido. He chronicled the long and bone-weary tale of their journeys from Troy and the many stops in Greece. Lending a sympathetic ear, she allowed them to stay until they recovered.

Dido was the stunning widowed queen. Her brother had previously murdered her husband, Sychaeus, leaving her alone to rule. While she was building the new laws of her city, she fell in love with Aeneas.

Aeneas and Dido were madly in love. After having relations in a cave during a rainstorm, she proposed to Aeneas, indicating that their act of love essentially made him king. Aeneas, weary and longing for a place to settle, initially agreed to the proposition. He lived with her for a year before abruptly leaving.

Jupiter's Nudge

Jupiter was ever watchful over Aeneas while he remained in Carthage. To his dismay, Aeneas was distracted by the beautiful queen and the life she promised him. However, Carthage was not the destiny of Aeneas. Concerned, he instructed Mercury to remind the prior Trojan of his duty to found a new civilization. Mercury obliged and met Aeneas, advising him to continue on his journey.

Reluctant to leave, he prepared his fellow crew members to set sail. In his haste, he did not tell his new love of his plan to leave; he could not bear to see her upset. He pressed forward, leaving Carthage and Dido.

Dido soon found out that he, and the rest of the Aeneads, had left without saying a final farewell. Feeling enraged and inconsolably distraught, she threw herself atop a still-burning funeral pyre.

While she burned to death, she cursed the Trojans and their eventual home. Her curse, it was widely believed, was the cause of the conflict between the Carthaginians and Romans called the Punic Wars.

Sicily Revisited, Cumae, and the Underworld

Since a year had passed in Carthage, the Aeneads decided to stop at Sicily in remembrance of Anchises, the father of Aeneas. To honor his father, they held another round of Trojan Games. While everyone appeared to enjoy themselves at first, Juno snuck fear into the women by setting ablaze their ships. Many attempts were made to stop the ships from burning; nevertheless, most of them were either badly damaged, beyond repair, or sank into the sea. Many of the women demanded that they stay in Sicily. To then further demoralize Aeneas, many others decided they also wanted to stay in Sicily. The remaining few of the Aeneads drifted onward to their next stop: Cumae.

Cumae was located about 12 miles west of present-day Naples and was home to the prophetess named Sibyl. Decrepit with old age, she was roughly seven hundred years old. She foresaw his arrival and greeted him at the temple of Apollo before granting his wish of seeing his father again. Aeneas was given the two difficult tasks of fetching a golden bough as a gift to Proserpina and burying a musician by the name of Misenus. The Aeneads buried the musician while he grasped two golden boughs. Aeneas and Sibyl then entered the Underworld.

Upon entering the Underworld, he and Sibyl crossed the River Styx on the ferry known as Charon. Sibyl gave a drugged cake to Cerberus, the three-headed wolf beast and guardian of the Underworld. Sibyl showed him the depths of Tartarus, the Hell of the ancient Romans, where he caught a glimpse of men being tortured and heard their agonizing screams.

Aeneas placed the golden bough in front of Pluto's throne, granting him access to Elysium, the Roman equivalent of Heaven. In Elysium, Aeneas finally saw his father and attempted to hug him. Instead, the spirit of his father wisped out of the embrace. Anchises, however, spoke to Aeneas, reminding him of his destiny. Instructing Aeneas to drink from the river of forgetfulness called Lethe, Anchises showed him the promise of his descendants of the new city. The faces of Romulus, Julius Caesar, Emperor Augustus, and many others showed themselves to him. Rejoicing, he left the realm of the Underworld and ascended to earth.

The War Over Latium

Finally, almost ten years after the sacking of Troy, Aeneas and his men reached the Tiber River. Initially rejoicing at the site of their future home, they did not realize their arrival would be the cause of another war, but this time over who would marry the daughter of King Latium.

Upon the arrival of the Aeneads, they and Turnus, a rival leader of the Rutuli, engaged in war. It was prophesied for Lavinia, the daughter of King Latium and his wife Queen Amata, to marry a foreign man of godly descent. King Latium abided by this prophecy, but Turnus wanted to marry her instead.

The marriage of Turnus and Lavinia was threatened by the arrival of the Aeneads; many Italians including Queen Amata were concerned. Originally the marriage to Turnus would have brought the peoples of Latius and the Rutili together. The threat of another man—a foreigner, no less—was unthinkable. King Latium held steadfast in his belief in the prophecy and aided the Aeneads.

The aid of King Latium was not the only help Aeneas received. With the rising conflict, Venus pleaded to her husband Vulcan to fashion armor for her son. Vulcan granted her request, and Aeneas received armor and a shield depicting the future of his people.

Juno also interfered with the hearts and minds of the Italians. She whispered into the ear of Turnus, promising glory and the hand of Lavinia if he won the war against the Aeneads. He obliged and continued to fight.

The war raged, causing the deaths of many friends close to both Aeneas and Turnus. A temporary truce was agreed upon, with Aeneas and Turnus facing off in one-on-one combat. Turnus agreed that if Aeneas should win, he would also win the right to marry Lavinia.

Aeneas and Turnus engaged in combat. The fighting was dirty and bloody, and all was lost for Aeneas. Gloating, Turnus relished in the glory that he was about to end the prophecy and marry the princess. Aeneas, however, was not so easily defeated. Upon catching sight of the sword of a fallen comrade in this war, anger surged through him. He pinned down Turnus and killed him.

The Prophecy Fulfilled

With the death of Turnus, Aeneas was now free to marry Lavinia. The kingdom entered an era of peace and prosperity under the rule of Aeneas. Jupiter eventually convinced Juno to end her war with Aeneas. Knowing she had lost, she ceased her constant warmongering against him.

Virgil's famous poem ends with the death of Turnus, and not much else is known about the death of Aeneas. Some retellings of the myth depict Aeneas as dying from the wounds in his last battle, while others imagine him living a long and full life after the marriage to Lavinia.

Conclusion

This origin myth of the land of Rome set the stage for the myths of Romulus and Remus, who are believed to be the founders of the great city. This epic tale encompassed twelve books in Virgil's *The Aeneid*, showcasing the resilience of a singular man and his tenacity to settle his people. While he had many deities helping him, he was portrayed as a great soldier and a strong leader, the epitome of life as a Roman citizen. With Aeneas and his ancestry, the myth proved the land itself to be rooted in the Roman pantheon of the gods.

Chapter 5: Rome: The Namesake of Romulus

Of all the Roman stories, the myth of Romulus and Remus is the most famous. The story introduces the ancient civilization and city of Rome, named after Romulus. With this new city, a vast empire that lasted for over a thousand years was born. The city of Rome is currently one of the most visited places in the world due to its rich culture and the amount of history spanning across millennia.

Cracks in the Foundation

In order to understand the legend of the twins, a trip to the past is necessary. After Aeneas passed away, his son Ascanius founded a city on Alba Longa. This city was southeast of the eventual city of Rome. There, his descendants rose and fell as the city grew.

It was around the eighth century BCE when the cracks of the foundation widened into chasms. Their king, Numitor, was in power when his brother Amulius plotted a coup against him, seizing control over Alba Longa.

The kingdom was now in chaos. After Amulius took the seat of power over the kingdom, he killed Numitor's only son and sent his daughter, Rhea Silvia, to become a priestess of Vesta, the goddess of the hearth. This was to prevent any retribution and retaliation from the family in the future. As a priestess, Rhea Silva was to remain a virgin for at least 30 years. The fact she was not to bear any children gave him hope of the future of ruling the kingdom.

The Birth of the Twins

As with most myths, there are varying details of the conception of Romulus and Remus. Some sources claimed that Rhea was raped by the Roman god Mars in the sacred wood behind the temple of Vesta; others claim it was a consensual meeting in a sacred grove dedicated to the Roman god. There are other claims that she was impregnated by an unknown stranger, and therefore, the twins are of no godly lineage. To keep it simple, this book will cover the rape of Rhea storyline.

The Roman god of war, Mars, spotted Rhea Silva in the sacred wood behind the temple. She was performing her sacred duties of maintaining the everlasting fire of Vesta when the god stumbled across her. Enticed by her beauty and quiet demeanor, he raped and impregnated her. She later gave birth to her twin sons, Romulus, and Remus.

King Amulius heard of the rape and the birth of the children. Enraged and terrified of the consequences, he ordered them to be thrown into the Tiber River. The boys were ripped from their mother's arms by guards following the direct orders of the king and imprisoned her for her indiscretion. They were then entrusted to a servant to toss them into the river.

The servant pitied the children and placed them in a basket on the bank of the river, hoping someone would find them and they would be spared. Due to torrential rain and flood, the children were swept away in the basket. The god of the river, Tiberius, rescued them and allowed them to drift ashore safely.

Lupa and Faustulus

A lonely she-wolf by the name of Lupa, believed to be Mars in disguise, brought the crying children back to her cave, where they suckled from her teat. She protected and fed the twins until the next stop in their saga. The famous bronze statue of the twins suckling from her teat is still in the Capitoline Museum today, an important symbol of the birth of Rome. It is also interesting to note that the Latin word for *lupa* means "prostitute". Some sources, though the myth of an actual she-wolf is more compelling, believe that the *lupa* was a lonely prostitute.

Faustulus, a local shepherd who guarded the herd of Amulius, walked along the forest when he heard the cries of infants. The cries led him to a cave in the she-wolf's lair, where he found the twins crying from hunger. Faustulus pitied the children and brought them home to his wife, Acca Larentia. The shepherd and his wife raised the sons as their own, unaware of their lineage and claim to the throne.

The boys were raised as farmers, and they helped the man they presumed to be their father farm the land and care for the farm animals. As the boys grew into men, they were protectors of the flock, battling predators and thieves alike. Their courage and ferocity earned them a reputation among the other shepherds. They were known to be leaders of their community with an active role in politics. Although not politicians, they often were seen in heated debates between the supporters of Amulius and Numitor. The supporters were shepherds, same as the twins, but their political views caused a fight to break out. The fighting ended with the imprisonment of Remus in Alta Longa, the place of their birth.

After Remus was taken, Romulus jumped into action. He led a band of other shepherds to break Remus out of jail. He knew the king would not favor Remus for speaking out against him; so, the trip to Alba Longa was a must.

The Death of Amulius, Fratricide, and the Birth of Rome

Upon Remus's arrival at Alba Longa, he was taken to Numitor to be sentenced. Numitor, however, recognized Remus as his grandson. When Romulus came to free Remus, Remus informed his brother of their surprise lineage. After learning of their heritage, Romulus and Remus devised a plan to rid of their great-uncle, Amulius. While it is not known who dealt the final killing blow, they overthrew and killed him.

After the death of Amulius, Romulus and Remus restored the kingdom to the rightful king, their grandfather Numitor. Numitor, grateful for the restoring of the kingdom, offered for them to rule jointly over Alba Longa. They refused the offer. They set off to where they were rescued by the she-wolf, the creature who had given them new life to found a new city of their own.

Romulus and Remus, however, could not agree on the location of the new city. Begging for the help of the gods, they waited on a sign for a preference on the location. Romulus settled on Palatine Hill, near the she-wolf's cave, while Remus chose the Aventine Hill.

The gods sent two separate flocks of birds to each of the brothers. Remus noticed a flock of six birds was on the horizon and claimed to see them first. Romulus, on the other hand, glimpsed a flock of twelve birds.

Romulus believed that since he saw the higher number and because the number twelve was related to the number of main gods in the Roman pantheon, he argued that Palatine Hill was the correct choice. Meanwhile, Remus argued that because he had seen the flock of six birds first, the Aventine Hill was the divine choice.

Romulus had built a wall around his settlement despite never fully committing to an agreement. In a fit of rage, Remus jumped over the wall to his brother's settlement. He and Romulus were locked in a battle. Whether by accident or on purpose, Romulus killed Remus, committing fratricide. It was evident that Romulus was favored by the deities.

After the death of Remus, the settlement Romulus had built was then called Rome after himself. The founding date of Rome was April 21, 753 BCE, the day Romulus declared himself king. He was Rome's first of seven kings before the rise of the Roman Empire. With the new kingdom, he recruited some of the shepherds and invited them to live in Rome with him. This invitation caused another myth to follow suit: the rape of the Sabine women.

The Rape of the Sabine Women

While the thought of founding a new kingdom was exciting, it had one major flaw. There were no women in the group Romulus had invited. No women meant it was impossible to have any kind of future for the kingdom. In an attempt to broaden the gene pool, the city accepted refugees and exiles from the surrounding kingdoms. While there were some additions, it was not enough to sustain the population. In a desperate attempt to solve the issue, he asked the neighboring kingdoms to give the Romans some of their women in order to increase the population. None of them agreed.

The requests of the Romans had reached the Sabine kingdom ruled by King Titus Tatius. The king then banned the Roman men from entering their walls. Women were forbidden to take a Roman's hand in marriage.

Romulus, however, hatched a plan. Under the pretense of conducting games in the name of Neptune, Romulus and his men planned and hosted the games in Rome but had an ulterior motive. Romulus, and the rest of the Senate, agreed to invite not only the Sabines, but other neighboring towns and kingdoms.

The day of the games arrived, bringing in many visitors who wished to see the new kingdom. The games began. Many spectators from neighboring lands sat around and watched the games take place. With the signal from their Romulus, the men began to abduct the Sabine women. Their tasks also included fighting off the fathers and brothers of the women.

A total of 30 women were forcibly taken from their homes. Most of them were believed to be virgins with the exception of the future wife of Romulus by the name of Hersilia who was already married. A war brewed under the surface of this abduction.

With the abduction of the women, King Titus declared war on the Romans and marched an army to the walls of the city. With the help of Tarpea, a Roman woman who was seduced by King Titan's wealth and the promise of safety, they opened the gates to Rome. Sadly for her, she was crushed to death by the shields of the Sabines as they broke through the gates.

The battle for the Sabine women ensued. In a desperate plea for the cease of further bloodshed, the women who were abducted agreed to stay in Rome along with their families, but they were not to be harmed. King Titus reluctantly agreed to the temporary truce. Romulus then implored for the women to marry the men of Rome.

The boldness of the abduction led to many other wars between the Romans and Sabines, as well as other neighboring kingdoms who saw the growing city of Rome as a threat. Over time, these kingdoms were conquered and merged with Rome.

The Death of Romulus

The death of Romulus is the final myth. In his final years, Romulus had gained a massive kingdom and sired the future kings and other rulers of Rome. During a rough storm, Romulus disappeared near the Tiber River. It was widely speculated that Romulus was then transformed into the god Quirinus. Not much is known about the deity, but it was assumed the god was similar to Mars.

Conclusion of the Founding of Rome

The founding of Rome and the myths that revolved around it were widely accepted, and as such, it was believed by the Romans that the land had a deep connection with the gods. Aeneas was a direct result of a coupling between Venus and a mortal man; Romulus and Remus were a result of a coupling between Mars and a mortal woman. The connection at the time was undeniable; Rome was the culmination of two main deities of the Roman pantheon. Rome was where the gods had intended for their people to grow and thrive in Italy. Because the gods favored this location, the people of Rome expanded well over millennia and through many European and some Asian cultures of today.

The ancient Romans effectively illustrated through Virgil's epic poem and the stories of Romulus and Remus how the gods not only shaped the present with their decisions, but also the future. Venus and Mars were both responsible for curating one of the largest empires the world had ever seen. They were ruling deities of two solid, natural, fearsome forces: love and war.

Chapter 6: Jupiter and the Bee

The next chapters will deal exclusively with the gods of the Roman pantheon and their stories. Many of these myths may have Greek counterparts, as they stemmed from Greek mythology and were adapted to the belief systems and behaviors of the Romans. While the Greek and Roman pantheons, for the most part, were essentially the same, there were some deities that were strictly Roman. Through various ancient texts, pictures, and even word of mouth, the myths have evolved and changed over time.

Jupiter and the Bee is one of the most common myths surrounding Jupiter. It is a tale of vengeance and sweetness, reminding those who heard the fable to be wary of what they wish for. The myth explained a bee's need for a stinger with the promise of death if used.

The Queen Bee and Her Honey

A bee returned to her home after the exhausting task of collecting pollen. Ready for a night of sleep, she investigated her hive as she did every night beforehand. As soon as she entered her hive, she knew something was off. As she inspected closer, claw marks were gouged in the very fabric of her hive. She then realized that her precious honey was stolen.

Any time she would produce any honey, a mortal or an animal came in and stole from her. She would spend her day repairing the destruction left behind by whatever creature decided to raid her home that day.

This little bee was not the only one to have this problem with the creatures who wandered in the forest. In between the bears and mortals, there was no reprieve from her plight. No amount of buzzing in their faces would prevent them from reaching into her hive and pulling out the sweet nectar from her home. She needed something to defend herself. A stinger on her back end, perhaps.

Pleased with idea, she prayed often for a stinger, but none of the gods ever responded. They were usually too busy getting themselves into trouble with each other, meddling with the mortals, or both. The gods did not care a bit about her troubles. It was time to take her troubles to them.

The Plea

The queen only knew where Jupiter presided, so she grabbed some of her sweet, delectable honey and flew off to find him. When she found Jupiter in heaven, she buzzed around him until she caught his attention.

Curious, he asked what it was she wanted. She then presented the honey as a gift. Jupiter graciously took a small dab of honey on his pointer finger and tasted it. The god relished in its sweetness, an unexpected treat from an unexpected source. Knowing this was a barter, he asked the queen bee what she needed of him.

Trembling in fear, the queen spoke in a small but firm voice. She explained how tired she was of animals and humans alike, who were constantly destroying her hive in search of honey. She was in a constant state of repair and rebuild, but she needed to harvest the honey for her own children to grow.

She asked Jupiter for a weapon.

Amused, he considered granting her wish. After all, the sweetness of the honey would always attract thieves and unwanted destruction. But Jupiter, greedy for more, asked for more honey because the taste was so delectable.

In return, the queen asked for, more specifically, a stinger.

The Anger of Jupiter

When the queen bee, still trembling in fear but maintaining her composure under the watchful gaze of the god, asked for a stinger, Jupiter's face distorted in shock, disbelief, and anger. He accused her of using the weapon to sting the gods. His wrath was to be feared, and the bees were no exception.

The bee was so frightened, but she tried to still explain the need for her protection, explaining that her kind would not purposely sting anyone or anything. Jupiter, however, was not listening and so she blindly buzzed in the direction opposite of Jupiter only to run into Juno, who had been listening the entire time.

Jupiter gave the rest of his honey to Juno. She then looked at him, with a questioning expression on her face. Her gaze, once burning with curiosity, melted into pleasure. She was not expecting the honey to taste as good as it did.

She agreed with Jupiter and the queen bee: The honey was a gift that needed to be protected. She urged her husband to grant the bee's request and to give every bee a stinger. He granted the wish with the wave of his hand. She was now adorned with the stinger she desperately needed.

Repercussions

Before the bee was sent on her way, Jupiter said that the price of a stinger for every bee came with a cost. If the bee should ever use it, she would lose her stinger and die. Disheartened, she returned to earth while the other bees anxiously waited for her.

The queen bee did not receive the news well. She hid in her hive for two days while the other bees were showing off their stingers to one another. She knew the sounds of rejoicing would end in the sound of hatred.

Reluctantly, she emerged from her hive with a gentle coaxing from another bee. She informed all of them that the gift could be a curse. If they used their stingers, they would perish. The choice was either to share the honey or protect it by stinging the aggressor and dying.

The bees were loyal to her and gave her their support. They knew she had done her best, and that she had their best interests at heart. One of the bees gave the hopeful impression that perhaps the deal would not last and would eventually fade away into oblivion.

Unfortunately, the hopes of the bees were in vain. To this day, if a bee decides to use her stinger in protection, it will die.

Conclusion

While the main lesson of this myth is "to be careful what you wish for," it also explains the bee's phenomenal ability to sting others and sacrifice itself in order to protect its hive. The Romans used myths and legends to create lessons and stories based on their values and traits. The Romans could be very unforgiving and violent while full of love for their country, and would protect it at any cost, similar to the queen bee in this myth.

Chapter 7: The Reason of the Changing Seasons

The myth of Pluto and Proserpina is a riveting tale of a mother's heartbreak and fury, a kidnapping, and an unwanted marriage. This myth has several variations to it, as with most of the Roman and Greek myths, which is the result of translations and oral storytelling.

Some of the myths portray Ceres as an overprotective mother, with Pluto and Jupiter teaming up to allow Proserpina a sense of freedom. A few suggest that Cupid, the god of love, shot Pluto with a golden-tipped arrow, causing him to fall in love with the first person he saw. No matter the inciting incident of the myth, the story essentially remains the same.

Ceres and Proserpina

Ceres, the goddess of agriculture, often visited Sicily with her daughter Proserpina. The two goddesses often walked together, and the flowers grew, and birds sang in their wake. A train of maidens followed behind both goddesses, laughing and frolicking in the lush green hills dotted with flowers. The picturesque landscape was the favorite of the goddess Ceres—it presented an escape from the sometimes harsh reality of being a god.

Jupiter was Proserpina's father, but she was much closer to her mother. She loved the scent of blooming flowers and the greenery of the plants around her. Just like her mother, Proserpina felt at home in the groves of trees and fields of flowers. She tended to the plants with a high degree of gentleness and compassion. Nymphs and maidens danced around her, relishing in the carefree nature of the land.

Pluto's Plight, Cupid's Solution

Pluto was desperate for a queen. After repeated trial and error of finding a goddess to share the throne with him, it was time for a change in approach. Cupid, the god of love, sympathized with the downtrodden Pluto. As Pluto wandered the overworld in his dark carriage pulled by horses as black as night, Cupid shot him with a golden arrow fashioned by Venus herself.

His heart unnaturally spilled over with adoration for an unknown woman after he heard a mystical humming in the trees nearby. Intrigued, he had his horses wait on the side of the path and entered the meadow. His heart burst through his chest at the wonderment in front of him. He stood in the shadows and waited, simply observing his newfound love. He could not help but think her beauty and youth would breathe new life into the realm of the dead.

Proserpina sat with some nymphs in a meadow of fully bloomed flowers; the fragrances of orchids and carnations lingered in the air. Weary from her labors of tending the earth, she picked a host of flowers and stalks of grass. She weaved them into a floral crown for her mother, humming a tune to herself as she worked.

Help! Let Me Go!

Pluto could no longer control his urges. He shifted his weight as he prepared to swoop her in his arms. Twigs crackled under his feet. The strikingly beautiful Proserpina heard the subtle noise, but before she could move or speak, she was in the arms of another god. She knew of him, but could not place his name. Instead, she screamed, pleading for someone to help her.

The nymphs who had surrounded her previously stayed rooted in one place. They knew who he was. Fearful of the darkness and his reason for appearing in the world of the living, they trembled at the sight of him and watched in horror as he carried away Proserpina. After realizing their mistake, they took off after the immortals.

The god threw her into his carriage and spurred on the horses. Her screams started to attract the attention of passersby and the nymphs who trailed behind him. To prevent Ceres from snatching away his prize, he whipped the horses harder.

Eventually, he fled to the edge of the Cyane River, but the river knew of Pluto's intent. It swelled and thrashed at the god and his horses, who made a vain attempt to cross the river. The river was too powerful, so he would have to turn around. He knew Ceres would try to find him if he were to move in the other direction. At a crossroad, he plunged his trusty trident into the ground, splitting it to make way for his entrance into the Underworld.

The Dedication of a Mother

Ceres returned from her duties to the meadow where Proserpina liked to spend her time. She had once told Ceres it was her favorite place in the world; that nothing could ever compare to the stillness and peace of the meadow.

When Ceres appeared in the meadow, ready to call home her daughter, she stared at the empty spot. Proserpina was not there. She called out her daughter's name, but there was no response. In the spot where unbeknownst to her the abduction took place, the only evidence remaining was scattered petals strewn across the ground.

The flowers rooted beside her started to yellow, then darkened into a deep brown as the plants died. The immediate area around

Ceres began to wilt. The darkening of the plants spread out around her like a disease. The trees dropped their leaves as if bowing their heads and grieving with Ceres.

For several years, Ceres roamed the earth in search of her daughter. Everywhere she went, the plants around her suffered a terrible fate. The humans were now in the middle of famine; many people died from lack of food. The Underworld was now busy greeting the starved souls into their respected realms.

The Guidance from a Nymph

Ceres had returned to Sicily from yet another trip around the world. Her spirit crushed, she wept at the last place she had seen her precious daughter. A nymph named Arethusa had seen the goddess weeping and explained that she witnessed Proserpina in the Underworld. Not as a prisoner, but instead sitting on the throne beside Pluto.

A gleam of hope shone from Ceres for the first time in many years. She had scoured the earth in a vain attempt to find a clue to aid in the disappearance of her daughter. Now that she knew the fate of her daughter, it was time for action.

The goddess thanked Arethusa for her observation and enlisted the help of Jupiter, her brother, and the father of Proserpina. He agreed to a rescue of the goddess as long as she had not consumed anything in the Underworld. If anything was eaten by a mortal or god in the Underworld, they were not allowed to leave. The gods were in favor of this plan because of the immense famine the humans were suffering, as it meant they were unable to give proper sacrifices to the gods.

Proserpina and the Pomegranate

Jupiter sent Mercury and Ceres to the realm of the dead with a message to deliver. The gods pleaded for the return of Proserpina to the overworld to her mother, where she belonged. Pluto replied that he had no malicious intent behind her kidnapping; he only wanted to love and please her. Ceres, however, did not care in the slightest. She only wanted her daughter back.

Mercury told Pluto of the demands of her return; Pluto had sworn she did not eat anything from his realm. He, and the rest of the Roman pantheon, knew of the consequences of eating from the Underworld.

During her stint in the Underworld, Proserpina grew to care for the spirits in Elysium. She now had a sense of honor and purpose, something she realized she was lacking beforehand. She missed her mother, of course, but the independence and freedom allowed her to experience more of what life had to offer.

As she listened to the exchange, she plucked a pomegranate off the tree and took a bite. The fruit was deliciously sweet and ripe. Its juices dripped down her chin.

Pluto had come to fetch her at last, but he discovered a bite out of the pomegranate in her hand. Ceres and Mercury followed and discovered the scene for themselves. Pluto glimpsed inside the pomegranate to discover there were six seeds. His compromise was for six months of the year, one for each seed, she would remain in the Underworld, and for the other six she would return to the overworld.

Ceres accepted the conditions; she was only concerned that she could have her daughter with her again. When she embraced Proserpina for the first time in many years, the damage to the foliage of the earth reversed.

The Changing of the Seasons

For the six months while Proserpina was on earth with her mother, spring and summer had arrived. The flowers bloomed and the trees grew, bringing with it the promise of crops for the humans and the frequent sacrifices to the gods. New life presented itself in the grass and the trees; the rebirth of the world was on its way. The world was in balance again.

When Proserpina returned to the Underworld, Ceres dived into a deep depression. The crops wilted and the trees shed their leaves as if crying alongside her. So, Ceres roamed the world, biding her time until she could see her wonderful daughter again.

Conclusion

The main purpose of the myth was the rationalization of the changes in season. Before humans understood why the seasons changed, it was commonplace for stories to be invented to explain the phenomena of the universe. The result was these stories turned into widespread myths that were accepted by the Romans. Gods and goddesses, they believed, roamed and watched over them.

Chapter 8: The Myth of Jupiter and Io

The myth of Jupiter and Io is one of the many stories in which Jupiter, king of the gods, was unfaithful to his wife Juno. The resulting jealousy and deceit of the characters in the myths was something that the citizens of Ancient Rome could relate to and understand. It was believed that, even though the gods were immortal, they had their whims and flaws, just as humans did. Io, however, managed to escape and live a full, happy life, unlike many others who were lusted after by Jupiter.

Io, the Priestess of Juno

Io was the daughter of one of the minor river gods, Inachus, and was the priestess of Juno. She faithfully carried out her duties every day, which resulted in the favor of the goddess. One day after finishing her duties for the day, she took a break by one of the rivers and lay on the bank. It was a hot summer day, and she was exhausted from her duties. She enjoyed the gurgling of the river and the birds chirping nearby.

As with all of the lovers of Jupiter, Io was beautiful, one of the most beautiful women of Rome. She did not escape the gaze of Jupiter, and trouble soon began to brew.

Jupiter, The Dark Cloud of Infidelity

Jupiter was disguised in a dark cloud the first time he saw Io. As he drifted over the sun, he looked down at Io laying on the bank of the river, gleaming from sweat from the heat of the day. Her beauty was inconceivable. Immediately, he fell into lust. He needed to talk to this mortal goddess.

He morphed into his mortal form and struck up a conversation with Io. He made no attempts to disguise who he was, as he opened the exchange by wooing her and informing her of his name.

Io, understandably, was flattered. It was uncommon for a god to speak directly with a mortal, and rare for a god to converse with a priestess not associated with his own temple. He was also the king of the gods, so she was taken aback at how forward he was with her. After a while, she also wanted to be with the king.

They agreed to meet on a regular basis. Since the priestess knew that she was going against the wishes of the goddess she served, she was careful to not give anything away. In their meetups, Jupiter disguised himself as a black cloud.

Juno's Suspicion

Juno was no stranger to the wandering eyes of her husband. With more affairs than she could count, her jealousy had reached levels that were often out of her control.

She was aware that her husband left their palace at the same time every day and hung low over a certain section of Rome near her temple. Growing ever more suspicious, she decided to one day follow him and catch him in the act.

Jupiter was well aware of the jealousy of his wife. As the meetings with Io became more frequent and he spent longer stints of time away from his home, he came up with a clever solution. He knew his wife would try to catch him in the act. He kept a watchful eye out for her. One day, Jupiter saw that his wife was on her way. With the consent of his lover, he turned Io into a white cow who grazed on the bank of the river. He wanted to protect Io from the wrath of Juno.

The dark cloud of Jupiter hung over the cow as she grazed when Juno arrived. Juno, however, was no fool. After making remarks about the beauty and uniqueness of the cow, she asked Jupiter to give it to her as a gift. This cow was suspiciously under the great care of Jupiter; and she had a hunch as to why.

Jupiter knew that he could not refuse to give her the priestess-turned-cow. In order to hide his infidelity and his lover, he agreed to give her the cow. Knowing he was defeated for now and his secret was still safe, he left and went back to the palace.

Juno now had the upper hand. She sent the cow off with her ever-loyal servant, Argus, who had 100 eyes. The eyes rarely ever closed all at once; she knew that Argus would prevent any attempt of an escape. With Argus having constant surveillance of the cow, Juno believed the affair was over.

Mercury and Argus: The Many Tales of Boredom

When Jupiter found out what Juno had done to his lover, he was distraught. He felt guilty over keeping Io in that form for all eternity. After all, it was not her fault he had come to her with promises he could never keep. In his remorse, Jupiter asked for help from his son Mercury. His son listened to his tale, and he decided to help his father free the priestess.

Mercury walked up to Argus and sat down with the servant. Argus, who did not receive many visitors, welcomed the god at first. Mercury told tales of intrigue, trying to hold the attention of the creature. His silver tongue recounted many tales, and he went on tangents and rants about the business of the gods and mortals. As he gossiped and told Argus stories that had no point and made no sense, the creature drifted off to sleep.

He killed the beast as it slept and freed Io, who was still metamorphosed into a cow. Now free, she wandered around the countryside, waiting for Jupiter to turn her back into her previous mortal form.

The Vow of Jupiter

Once Juno discovered the treachery of Mercury and Jupiter, her wrath unfolded. In her misery and as a punishment, she unleashed a gadfly to sting the priestess for the rest of eternity. To honor her fallen servant, she fused her most beloved bird with the many eyes of Argus. The resulting animal was a beautifully ornate bird now known as a peacock, with its ever-watchful gaze

Io ran away from the fly as fast as she could, but the gadfly still was able to painfully sting her. She never felt any relief from the stings; the gadfly always found her, no matter how much she hid from it.

Jupiter, remorseful that Io was the one to be punished instead of him, swore a vow to Juno. If she let the priestess go, he would never pursue the priestess for the rest of her life. He would let Io be.

Juno released her control of the gadfly, who left Io alone and flew away. Relieved that Juno had kept her word, he released Io from the imprisonment of the body of a cow. In the end, Jupiter kept his vow and never saw her again.

Io, The First Egyptian Goddess

Io was grateful for her chance to live inside her own body again. She no longer wanted to be with Jupiter; he was not worth the cost of her life or the wrath of his wife. She gathered her things and left Rome, seeking a new place to settle.

The former priestess found her new home to be in Egypt. While she was there, she caught the eye of the king of Egypt and became his wife. She spent the rest of her days in luxury, far away from the chaos that was Rome. When she passed away, she ascended to the heavens and became the first goddess of Egypt.

Conclusion

The ending of this myth was a quiet resolution with a happy ending for the priestess. Unlike most of the other lovers of Jupiter, she found herself better off than she was while living in Rome. The lesson to be received from this myth is to not fall headfirst into lust. Io and Jupiter illustrated the point that if someone is in a romantic coupling with another, do not get involved. Someone is bound to get hurt. Jupiter may be able to get away with the numerous lovers in myths, but the reality is much messier.

Chapter 9: Bacchus and Ariadne

Love was one of the most powerful forces in the Roman pantheon. With Venus as a main deity and with roots directly tied to the foundation of Rome, love in all its forms was an all-encompassing power. Rome possessed a violent past in both its historical and mythological contexts, but the Romans were also known for their penchant for romance.

The myth of Bacchus and Ariadne is one that is full of betrayal and the inevitability of love. Love came from an unexpected source, but the result was an everlasting, eternal coupling.

Bacchus and the Pirates

Bacchus was the god of wine, but he, like all the gods, could transform into varying likenesses. One of his abilities was the ability to grow vines heavy with grapes and orchards with ripe fruit on a whim.

Bacchus often wandered the world in various forms, and this day, he wanted to be in the form of a young, wealthy human to interact with some locals. He loved to party with the mortals, often offering wine and a wonderful time. This time he wore jewelry adorned with precious metals and jewels.

Pirates had spotted him from a distance and kidnapped him. They gagged him while binding his hands and feet together. Bacchus overheard the plans of hiding him for ransom as they tied him to the mast of their ship. As they sailed away, Bacchus began to formulate his own plan.

As night descended and the waters grew deep, Bacchus unleashed vines from deep on the ocean floor. They tangled themselves within the ship and strangled many of the men. Bacchus morphed into a lion, clawing and biting those who had kidnapped him. The rest of the pirates threw themselves overboard in an attempt to escape the destruction.

With no one left on the ship, Bacchus sailed for the island of Naxos, where his future lover awaited.

Ariadne and the Betrayal

Ariadne, the daughter of King Minos, was once the lover of Theseus, the slayer of the Minotaur. She had helped him, while betraying her father, to keep track of his location in the Labyrinth by giving him a ball of string. After he had slayed the Minotaur, he sailed to the island of Naxos to celebrate his victory.

In his haste to leave for the next adventure, he had left his beloved Ariadne on the island, where she often waited by the shore, anxious for his return. It was debated whether the abandonment was through an act of a god such as Minerva or if he had doubts of bringing a Cretian princess to become the queen of Athens. His motives could have been a combination of the two.

Surely, he had realized he had left her. *He would be back soon*, she thought. Months went by before she realized he was not coming back for her. She longed to be off the island and patiently waited for her chance of escape.

The Ancient Sleeping Beauty

Bacchus had the ship docked on the island once he landed. While wandering the island, he offered wine to the locals and had a band of merry men follow him everywhere he went. He had morphed back into the wealthy, young man on the way to the island. He and his band of recruits paraded around the island in search of something to occupy themselves with.

He found Ariadne fast asleep next to the shore, the waves gently kissing the land next to her. She had laid there for quite a while; her clothes were dirty as if she had not moved. Bacchus, as if Cupid had shot an arrow and struck him, fell instantly in love with her. He waited by her until she regained consciousness.

Ariadne awoke to find the god of wine hovering over her. Dazed, she slowly got to her feet with the help of Bacchus. She explained her heartbreak and the betrayal of her previous love, how he had left her on the island alone.

Bacchus, angry at Theseus but grateful he had left her, asked her to marry him. He promised her to never abandon her the way her previous love did, and would remain steadfast and faithful to her.

She gazed over his attire and his otherworldly beauty. She agreed to marry him, and Jupiter decided to grant her immortality. In regard to gifts given to the new bride and goddess, Venus had fashioned her a crown to celebrate the occasion, which then became a constellation called Corona.

Ariadne and Bacchus went on to have multiple children together, thus giving a happy ending to the story.

A Dark Variation

In some of the variations of the myths, it was believed that Bacchus himself had suggested that Theseus abandon his love. Listening to the god, he left Ariadne on the island.

In her grief, she had hanged herself and was sent to the Underworld to meet her fate in the Fields of Mourning. However, Bacchus rescued her from that fate, resurrected her, and married her.

Immortalization of Their Love

During the Renaissance Period, a painter by the name of Titius painted the scene of the meeting between Bacchus and Ariadne. In this scene, the chariot of Bacchus was pulled by two cheetahs, and he proposed to Ariadne. When she accepted, she became part of the North Constellation.

Conclusion

Even though most of Roman mythology and culture revolved around the fascination of death, every once in a while, there was a break from the chaos and a beautiful love story emerged. In the tale of Bacchus and Ariadne, the everlasting love was a pinnacle of romanticization that did not often involve much violence. It gave the hope of finding a new love after being abandoned, a theme that continues through today.

Chapter 10: Pluto and the River Styx

As the last chapter in the book, it ends with the explanation of the last stage in life: death. Pluto, the god of death and king of the realm, played a major role in the rituals of the afterlife.

Pluto was a minor god in the world of the Roman pantheon. The few myths that revolved around him were far and few in between. As the King of the Underworld, he commanded the respect, fear, and admiration of the Romans.

Not much is known about the true origin of the myth that revolved around the River Styx. However, the fable in this chapter is directly related to the customs and procedures observed following the death of citizens of Rome.

Pluto and the Underworld

After he, Jupiter, and Neptune overthrew their father Saturn, Pluto was assigned to reign over the dead. Clothed in the gloominess of the Underworld, he ruled with both fairness and cruelty. As with every god in the Roman pantheon, he was well-respected and feared by the mortal souls he reigned over. Pluto was King of the entirety of the land below earth. While most of the other gods held glamorous positions, the lord of the dead held one of the most critical.

The Romans believed that the life they led was related to the type of treatment they would receive in death. The most honorable received peace; the most horrific received eternal torture. The Underworld had at least four different levels: Tartarus, the Fields of Mourning, the Asphodel Meadows, and the Fields of Elysium.

Tartarus

The most well-known of the Underworld, Tartarus was a massive pit in the Underworld that housed and tortured the most despicable in life. Their punishments fit their crimes in the world of the living. The continual blood-curdling screams of agony were among the most noticeable features, aside from it being the most massive pit in the existence of the Roman fables.

The Fields of Mourning

The Fields of Mourning was reserved for those who wasted away in the grief of love. They wandered aimlessly in smoky mists across the fields. Those whose grief was so strong that they could never forget the cause of their eternal suffering resided here. For example, Virgil placed Dido, the lover of Aeneas, in this level.

The Asphodel Meadows

Not much was known about the meadows; it was believed to have souls who did neither extraordinary feats nor atrocities. The meadows were reserved for those who were ordinary and lived neutral, meaningless lives. The souls either faded away or awaited their return for reincarnation on earth.

The Fields of Elysium

The Fields of Elysium were only reserved for the best of the best. These were the souls of the exceptional mortals who earned their right to have a life free of aches and pains. The father of Aeneas was placed here by the three judges upon his arrival in the Underworld.

Charon and the River Styx

In order to cross the River Styx, or the River of the Dead, a toll must be paid upon death. It was the responsibility of the loved ones of the deceased to ensure the toll was paid. At the funeral arrangement and ritual, a golden coin was placed under the tongue or on top of the closed eyelids of the dead. Those who could not afford the toll were destined to roam in between the worlds, never belonging to either.

Upon death, the soul of the mortal was greeted by Mercury, who then led them to the River Styx. The ferryman, Charon, waited for them; they paid the toll if they could and crawled aboard the ferry.

Cerberus

After the long ferry ride across the river, the soul disembarked to find the guardian of the Underworld. Cerberus was a fearsome, three-headed beast of a dog who guarded the gates of the entrance to the Underworld. Everyone who entered the gates was allowed to stay. No one, however, was allowed to leave. His job was to ensure that no one left the Underworld, with a handful of exceptions, including Aeneas.

The Three Judges

Pluto may have been the king, but he delegated the daily tasks of where to place mortals to three judges. The panel of these three judges consisted of Rhadamanthus, a son of Jupiter and Europa; Minos, who was one of the brothers of Rhadamanthus; and Aeacus, who was the son of Jupiter and Aegina. The judges weighed the life of each mortal soul and placed them in the proper zone.

Conclusion

The beliefs surrounding the Roman and Grecian burial traditions and where their souls ended was an interesting way of looking at the relationship between death and the life a person had lived. Some of the rituals were similar to those of today, with the belief of an afterlife being a universal concept from both the past and present.

No matter how much time has passed, the Roman pantheon complete with its fables, myths, and legends, will continue to captivate and inspire those in modern times. While the myths themselves were entertaining, each myth had at least one theme and lesson to be learned. The legends were passed down from generation to generation through the surviving epic poems of Homer, author of *The Iliad* and *The Odyssey*, and Virgil. In modern times, these myths have become the inspiration for multiple movies, TV shows, and books.

I hope you have enjoyed learning about the fascinating world of Roman Mythology! I invite you to take a look at my other books on Amazon which cover the mythologies of several different ancient cultures, namely Greek, Norse, Celtic, and Egyptian.

References

Adhikari, S. (2018, January 12). Top 10 Popular and
    Fascinating Myths in Ancient Rome. *Ancient History Lists*.
    https://www.ancienthistorylists.com/rome-history/top-10-
    interesting-roman-mythology/

Aeneas |Myth & Family| Britannica. (n.d.). Retrieved July 5,
    2022, from https://www.britannica.com/topic/Aeneas

Alford, C. (2017, May 2). An Ancient Greek Love Story: Titian's
    Bacchus and Ariadne. *Nouvelle Art*.
    https://nouvelleartsite.wordpress.com/2017/05/02/an-
    ancient-greek-love-story-titians-bacchus-and-ariadne/

Anderson, W. Scovil (2020, May 18). *Aeneas. Encyclopedia
    Britannica*. https://www.britannica.com/topic/Aeneas

Ascanius | Roman mythology | Britannica. (n.d.). Retrieved
    July 4, 2022, from
    https://www.britannica.com/topic/Aeneas

Atsma, A. J. (2017). *NYX - Greek Primordial Goddess of the
    Night (Roman Nox)*.
    https://www.theoi.com/Protogenos/Nyx.html

Brigden, J. (n.d.). *Who were the major Roman gods and
    goddesses?* Sky HISTORY TV Channel. Retrieved July 2,

2022, from https://www.history.co.uk/articles/who-were-
the-major-roman-gods-and-goddesses

Cavazzi, F. (2021, December 17). *The Roman Pantheon of Gods*.
The Roman Empire. https://roman-
empire.net/religion/list-of-gods/

Claudia. (2021, October 8). *15 Famous Rome Myths And
Legends*. https://strictlyrome.com/famous-rome-myths-
and-legends/

Garcia, B. (2013, September 1). *Minotaur*. World History
Encyclopedia. https://www.worldhistory.org/Minotaur/

Geurber, H. A. (n.d.). *The full myth*. Proserpina and Pluto.
Retrieved July 6, 2022, from
http://proserpinaandpluto.weebly.com/the-full-myth.html

Gill, N. S. (2020, January 29). *Fall of Rome—Common
Theories and Causes*. ThoughtCo.
https://www.thoughtco.com/reasons-for-the-fall-of-rome-
118350

Grant, M. (2016, May 2). *Roman religion—Priests | Britannica*.
https://www.britannica.com/topic/Roman-religion/Beliefs-
practices-and-institutions

GreekMythology.com, T. Editors of Website (2021, April 08).
Ariadne. GreekMythology.com.

https://www.greekmythology.com/Myths/Mortals/Ariadne
/ariadne.html

GreekMythology.com, T. Editors of Website (2015, January 24).
Rhadamanthus. GreekMythology.com.
https://www.greekmythology.com/Myths/Figures/Rhadam
anthus/rhadamanthus.html

GreekMythology.com, T. Editors of Website (2021, April 08).
The Underworld. GreekMythology.com.
https://www.greekmythology.com/Myths/Places/The_Und
erworld/the_underworld.html

Heli, R. (2012). *Ancient Roman Holidays & Festivals at The
Detective & the Toga.*
https://www.histmyst.org/festivals.html

Journey of Aeneas—Citizendium. (2021, January 27).
https://en.citizendium.org/wiki/Journey_of_Aeneas

Kiran. (2022, May 11). Cassandra: The Trojan Priestess of
Apollo From Greek Mythology -. *Dreams and Mythology.*
https://dreamsandmythology.com/cassandra-greek-
mythology/

Land, G. (2021, September 1). *The 12 Gods and Goddesses of
Pagan Rome.* History Hit. https://www.historyhit.com/the-
gods-and-goddesses-of-pagan-rome/

Law, E. (2018, March 1). *Veni, Vidi, Vici: Origin of the Saying "I Came, I Saw, I Conquered."* Culture Trip. https://theculturetrip.com/europe/italy/articles/veni-vidi-vici-origin-of-the-saying-i-came-i-saw-i-conquered/

Marta. (2021, November 23). Roman Mythology: 18 most famous ancient Rome myths and legends you need to know. *Mama Loves Rome.* https://mamalovesrome.com/roman-mythology-and-legends/

Mythical Creatures. (n.d.). Roman Mythology. Retrieved July 3, 2022, from http://romanmythologyinfo.weebly.com/mythical-creatures.html

Professor Geller. (2016, October 26). *Ceres—Roman Goddess of Agriculture.* Mythology.Net. https://mythology.net/roman/roman-gods/ceres/

Professor Geller. (2016, November 18). *Faun—Roman Mythological Half Human Half Goat.* Mythology.Net. https://mythology.net/roman/roman-creatures/faun/

Professor Geller. (2016, November 1). *Vesta—Roman Virgin Goddess of Home and Family.* Mythology.Net. https://mythology.net/roman/roman-gods/vesta/

Singh, Y. (2022, February 22). *The Rise of Christianity in Ancient Rome*. https://historyten.com/roman/rise-christianity-ancient-rome/

The Underworld. (n.d.). Retrieved July 7, 2022, from https://www.greekmythology.com/Myths/Places/The_Underworld/the_underworld.html

Wasson, D. L. (2018, May 8). *Roman Mythology—World History Encyclopedia*. https://www.worldhistory.org/Roman_Mythology/

12 major Roman gods you need to know about! (2020, November 7). *Museum Facts*. https://www.museumfacts.co.uk/romans-gods/